SUPERWOMAN turns 40

by
Donna Schaper

San Diego, California
LuraMedia™

© Copyright 1988 LuraMedia
San Diego, California
International Copyright Secured
Publisher's Catalog Number LM612
Printed and Bound in the United States of America

LuraMedia
7060 Miramar Road
San Diego, CA 92121

Library of Congress Cataloging-in-Publication Data

Schaper, Donna.
    Superwoman turns 40 : the story of one woman's intentions to grow
up / by Donna Schaper.
        p.   cm. — (The Women's series)
    ISBN 0-931055-57-1 (pbk.)
    1. Schaper, Donna. 2. Women—United States—Biography.
3. Mothers—United States—Biography.   4. Success—United States.
I. Title.   II. Series: Women's series (San Diego, Calif.)
HQ1413.S33A3   1988
305.4'092'4—dc19
    [B]   88-25795
                                                                     CIP

**To Warren,
  my partner**

The Turning Point

I used to think that once I got really organized, I could then relax. I thought that peace was the purpose of constant haste, that I could be a person as soon as I mastered the art of being a man. That's why I got degrees, was ordained, climbed the ladder the institutional church let down, and became a success — in manly terms — by age 38.

Even though there were days I worked so hard that my kidneys tried to burst — because I did not have time to pee and produce — I assumed that my vigor would validate the continued success which my early success required. The worst thing about success turned out to be its need to succeed itself.

One child at 36 and then twins at 38 did not rattle my cage. Better management coupled with superb child care was my domestic creed.

I also used to think that women like me could have it all. I don't think so anymore. I've discovered that "all" is too much. "Everything" squeezes out time for "nothing," and "nothing" is the margin that anything requires to be good.

My life was all picture with no frame. "Superwoman Goes Home" was the title of a book I threatened to write late one night after a typically absurd day.

That was when I first cried during a meeting (something Geraldine Ferraro, by the way, is praised for having avoided). My tears were fear: What if all this organized effort made me like THEM? My 54-member board of directors had 53 men on it. Each was fast on the way to losing his capacity to care. Some had already lost it.

I needed a diet of work that nurtured instead of depleted. I needed exercises that kept the caring muscles alert. I needed to get back — or forward — to myself.

Cul-de-sac

Of course I considered the possibility of being a fly in their ointment. Of being different from men. Maybe of even changing the pattern of managerial isolation of selfishness . . . this superwoman rarely made small plans.

I didn't seem to notice that the women's movement of my youth had resulted in permission for women to become more like men. You know: hard choices, long hours, three-piece suits, and no spare time. The self had to be protected from a thousand assaults on its position. Women were now free to enjoy the preoccupation of the self with its power.

But I was too tired to do it all — to be them and to be me — so I muddled along, stuck in the old patterns of self-destruction that feminism had proposed to abandon. My attempt to care for others as well as myself — and to change me at the same time — was doomed to fail by the obvious, but not accepted, limits to my own energy.

Constitutionally unable NOT to care for my male co-workers, I became an astute analyst of their problems. I was their mom away from home. Even though I had left one marriage long ago in a refusal to mother a man my age, at work there were sons old enough to be my father.

The combination of the women's movement that failed me, my own fatigue, and my incapacity to distance male need resulted in ridiculous failure to achieve any of my plans to change the work place. There was no doubt that it was changing me: every one of my strategies was in the direction of caring less.

That's when I started to think about power again. This time I thought about how to get power to be a woman. I really didn't want to be a man.

Polish Surprises

Even in the midst of this most horrible time of my life, a few unsolicited gifts came my way. One was a Polish baby sitter who had the odd effect of renewing my interest in Solidarity. Thus, I was led to reading the poet Adam Michnik's letter from Gdansk. It made sense.

"What to do when you have no power?" he asks. First of all, don't validate THEIR power by acting like them. Don't want what they have. If you have no guns, don't use guns to get free. Besides, using guns only indicates that guns are important. And they are not. (Neither are penises.)

If you want to be free, act freely. Don't wait until after the Revolution to live. Live now.

There are all kinds of areas that totalitarian Poles and American men can't control — conversation, reading, community, whether we say the truth or not.

Culture, not politics, is a space that power doesn't have the time to control. Taking cultural power back will not change the work place. Eventually the issue of work and its constraints returns. But taking cultural power back WILL keep the work place from changing us.

Women's culture is what's missing now from the work place. In our haste to "make it" in the man's world, we have moved into their house. Some of us, at least, have to move out and take back what we gave away.

Size

Women's culture is too big a word for what I mean. All I'm saying is that caring is important. That other people are as important as ourselves. This has an oddly biblical ring, one not just available to the preacher. What would have happened if our movement had taught men to be more like women rather than teaching women to be more like men? Men who worked six hours, not ten. Husbands who understood child care as a chunk of their salary. Dishes that got done in a kitchen administered by two people. Birthday cards to in-laws as a male and female agenda. Children important to more than one kind of adult. Women mothered after puberty. Adults able to have friends after college. Secretaries free to take time "off" when they have a problem.

I don't know at what point these seismological shifts would result in banning the bomb or getting our sons out of uniforms. It's hard to say when women would have the time again to pee.

I don't know because I don't think like that. I'm not a big picture person. And I don't want to be one.

Big pictures are a big part of the problem. Power over my small pictures seemed to be the first step.

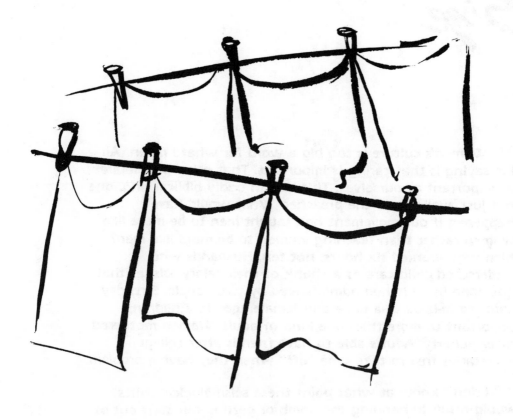

Budgets and Calendars

To get power to care meant I had to do something about my calendar and budget. Each seemed to be a world very much within my reach. Thank you, Michnik, for focusing my attention. Forgive me, if my freedoms trivialize your cause.

I prepared to quit my job and stay home. Fifteen years as a stranger in the strange land of work had taken its toll. I now had three children, and even six hours a day away from them hurt. It hurt in my stomach and in my arms. I wanted to be with them. Droning about policy, even high-level policy, caused my fingers to tap on table tops, my glance at the watch on my wrist to quicken. Surely these conversations were not as satisfying as my children's diapers.

But, then, more trouble.

My children's diapers weren't that satisfying either. My few hours a day with my three kids drove another part of me nutty. I worked 9 to 3 and 8 to 10 at this point in my life. One part of me had to go to work; another had to stay home.

Where I would be at any given hour suddenly seemed to be the simple part. The hard part was what I'd do or who I'd be in either place.

I had a lot of freedom to come to terms with.

Money

I had been continually bothered by what would happen to our budget if I quit work. How could we live without the upper bracket which our rental property and two incomes had accustomed us? We were already having trouble. Superwoman's death gave me a new perspective on this balderdash, too. Don't worry: I know how "rich" we were/are.

I learned that even a lot of money isn't enough. More than half of my salary paid for taxes and child care. Anxiety is always too expensive. My attachment to our current budget was a form of slavery. I cared about it so much that it was a master with a whip in its hand.

I needed something that money couldn't buy.

The first few days of freedom from our budget's appetite were exhilarating. After that I got a little stingy. I began to realize that relative poverty was an equal master to relative wealth.

I began to get very bored by the size of the financial decisions. Just looking at the calculator made me tired. I needed to understand that some of my fears were independent of wealth and poverty. They seemed to be mine no matter the amount in the checkbook.

More money or less money had no fundamental consequence when it came to maintaining my threatened capacity to care. The anxiety was present in either direction — either when giving away and spending, or when hoarding and keeping.

16

Children

I had also hoped that my taurus could be pinned on the double and mixed blessing of the twins. After all, they were and are a curve ball thrown at sanity. My two-year-old, of course, hated them, and I participated in the myth that mothering was the job of making everyone happy. Back to demythologizing.

But, on good nights, clicking our interfaith forks at the table to say our borrowed grace ("Good food, and lots of it, for everyone"), I would touch that joy given by sparkling eyes and would consider another pregnancy. I was only 38. And these children — Isaac, Katie, and Jacob — were so beautiful. Each one had a special way of making me deeply happy.

Was not their real rival my overdoing and overdoneness, not each other — or their number? Wasn't their rival my work misconstrued? And wasn't my work to love them? Of course, it was.

As threatened as my capacity to care had become, the failure never extended to them. Imperfectly, I loved them. Both the love and its imperfection kept my heart from becoming a stone.

Their forgiveness of my imperfection was so clear. I wondered why I couldn't do what they could.

Husband

Having decided that work itself or money itself was not the problem, I still had a few places beyond myself to consider. I may even have hoped at this stage that my husband was the problem. Facing either myself or my world still seemed too hard. Plus, I had gotten good at what the shrinks call "externalization." I had a major league self-interest in locating the cause of my waning ability to care in something other than me.

I discovered, much later, some external sources. But none had the face of my husband or male colleagues. The face I discovered was more systemic, non-personal: if it had eyes and hair, a lot would have been easier. Some of the problem was mine; I gave the systems power over me. But "they" had a life and power of their own. Imagine me, a trainer on systemic issues, finding it so hard to think systemically, for so long, about the sorrow in my life. Twenty lashes are my due — or at least being forbidden for six months from saying, "the personal is the political."

My husband: a smart, sexy misfit who lived with me with every ounce of his being and still couldn't protect me (damit) from me or my world. A full partner in dishes and diapers. Seriously. More like a good woman friend than a man-only, with notable exceptions to that in bed. My partner in this mess, moment by wasted moment. A Jew who helped me understand my Christianity. The victim of my frustration as my cope ran over. A great partner in childbirth. A Ph.D. in American history, which allowed him to understand the limits of my radicalism better than I. Through me, he developed the emotional side of the American stories he knew so well.

Was he part of the problem? Hell, no.

More Family

My parents are lower middle-class; his, upper. As a result, they are a split vote when it comes to our status. Split internally and externally, like most parents. Good to move up; bad to outshine. Class — of the impossible to measure economic, cultural, and educational variety — is one report card adult parents use for adult children.

My direction — of creating the space to ignore class, spiritually, or politically, or any way I could — was considered naïve by in-laws and mysterious to parents. Which is exactly what it was. Who said parents were dumb?

I couldn't afford to look for good grades anymore, even from parents. Nor could I afford the luxury of explaining myself.

Class would have to be a consequence and not the cause of my living.

It was amazing the number of resources I already had in husbands, parents, and children. Same was true of brothers, sisters, in-laws — although in recent years I've not had the time to enjoy their presence.

Like my children, my parents are known for their capacity to forgive.

Even More Family

My best time with my father was right after the end of my first marriage. On the way to the Buick place to get the car fixed, he informed me that he knew the real secret of my divorce. Breathless, I waited the word. The real secret, he said, was "women's lib." I had been influenced by it and didn't understand that women were below, not equal, to their husbands. (We had just left my mother with orders that she pick up his beer. I had objected and SHE had quieted me.)

Fortunately, I was able to assure him that women's lib was not the problem. It was he himself who had guaranteed my notion of equality. Coaching my softball team, cheering as I starred in basketball games, treating me as though I were the son he wanted. It had all sunk in.

But so did the limitations of being a woman, only those limits came much later, after I had already been formed by higher expectations.

Next time we go to the Buick place, I'll have to tell him the real secret of women's lib: it's letting yourself be a woman while demanding that the world treat you as though you were a man. It's a bit of a tightrope. My mother too often allowed the world and my father to treat her badly. She agreed to that mistreatment because she thought it was right. I, and my daughter, will have to extract different treatment. And we'll have to figure out what it is to be a woman while we get it.

Friends were likewise the victims of my overly full, empty calendar. I'd actually done better than most in maintaining the intimacies of my youth. But this superwoman had observed the fast track to loneliness as well as anyone else. Conversations with women friends had become less and less frequent as both they and I worshipped smaller gods. We had to make appointments with couples two or three weeks weeks in advance to eat an overly careful dinner together. Friends from afar got the mimeographed Christmas shout.

Even though conversations with friends from near and far were the things I most enjoyed, I let that abundance slip away. Why? Because I wanted to be like everyone else, and they wanted to be like everyone else — and all these everyones had bosses of calendar and budget that were psychological tyrants. Or maybe I was afraid to let my friends see who I'd become or to see who they'd become. It was all wrong.

Next to family, friends were and are my most coveted aspiration. There is nothing that stops me from achieving that community. Except a society that puts production over caring at every turn. A society that no one was forcing me to participate in. That mistake I seemed to be making all by myself.

My Terms at Work

Not to win battles or to see my colleagues as adversaries.

Not to be bored or boring.

Not to get stuck on abstractions; not to remain stuck on details.

To do my piece and not to schedule more.

To make my contribution and create space and time to appreciate the contributions of others; to play some other game than the turf-battle of competition.

To quit if I can't do these things, or to get fired in the process of trying them.

Not to call in sick under a pseudonym, like I've heard women do, so scared are they that the boss will think they have sickly children.

To care.

To sleep when I feel tired.

My Terms at Home

To be happy.

To care for my children.

To model for them happy, adult behavior; to give them the gift of a mother who has figured out her own life so they don't have to do that for her.

To mother them in partnership with work; to tell the truth about the "working woman," whatever that truth may be.

Quitting or continuing to work no longer seemed the issue of the day. That silly euphemism about "working outside the home" as a cute way of making the double point no longer seemed so cute. The real conflicts women face in their double work seemed acutely present to me, only these conflicts were wrapped in a larger blanket.

The calendar had a funny way of looking the same after I made these decisions; what was different was my perspective.

Super·Con

For a long time I wanted to title these reflections,
"Superwoman Goes Home: A Diet and Exercise Manifesto."
That proved too brazen. Superwoman does not go home, she
heads for home, back to values she should never have left;
exercising muscles of self and social reflection any democratic
citizen has; going on a diet which, like most, chooses certain
nourishments and avoids junk food. The trick in the brazen
title was the deserved ridicule of self-improvement: the
fantasy that by improving our self to youthful appearance
(via diet and exercise) we can feel better/good about our
spiritual and political homelessness. Here's a secret for you:
the soul and the society torment even thin bodies.

The soul's torment derives from its participation in the
society's false values. Busyness. Getting ahead. Legitimizing
our existence by doing things. The junk food of creating
distance from children, husband, family, and friends. The
permission we give society to tell us what to do. The
debasing of the right of a citizen to think for herself. Being a
silent partner with a society that undercuts caring through
systems of work, play, defense budgets, bombs, sexism, social
"services," and "therapies" for the maladjusted and the
misfit. Being a silent partner with a society where we are not
at home.

Lose Weight, Exercise More

The diet and exercise I needed were all about KEEPING the capacity to care that I thought was being stolen. What I discovered was that, far from being stolen, I was giving it away. My work was teaching me how to care only for myself and my limited turf, and I was much too good a student. I was starving myself by reducing association with family and friends. Somehow I thought I had to. But I was wrong. I didn't have to. Neither friends nor family wanted me to be a superwoman. My colleagues (at their best) didn't want that either. But my schizophrenia was deep: I heard voices. All the time. Advertisements. High School Teachers. Friends who still had a stake in the system. The voices of my loved ones sometimes borrowed these crazy voices and used them on me. The voices never stopped. But I could stop listening to them. I could even refine my ability to tell the difference between a healthy and a sick message. That's the exercise I needed much more than sit-ups. That program of exercise required a great deal of attention to diet. Time taken back from the sick environment of production and given to the healthy environments of caring. Obviously, they overlap.

Exercise was the discipline I needed to differentiate the layers. Community was the nourishment. Caring was the goal.

The Costs

I knew that opening up my battle with the world was not going to be easy. Or maybe it would be too easy. I was sure I could find a way to keep the difficulty index high.

You have to figure there will be tension: either the tension of being a square peg in a round hole, wearing hats and clothes that don't fit, or the tension of punching the invisible time card of production. I suppose I could have pulled the plug on the seductive advertising by becoming a nun and moving into an underground home in Mali — but I was too convinced of the goodness of my alternatives to bury them or me.

Tension was a given. What was different was setting the terms on which anxiety would sing its song.

Money may be a cost whenever it pleases; I'm now sure that it was not the issue. A harder loss was status; culture has a way of being explicit about who counts and how much. Three units of status seemed a pretty good trade for three units of freedom — or whatever the measurement finally becomes. See how well educated I am on the exchange rate?

I didn't set out to reduce risk. My purpose was and is to hook the risk to a star worth approaching.

The Middle of My Tether

My vows to slow things down and live in spiritual stability were failing. Three days after my abortion (yes, I got pregnant ten months after the twins were born), my Polish baby sitter's plans to marry an American to get a green card so she could bring her daughter to this country to rescue her from her ex-husband's threats to kidnap her from her parents were exposed to immigration by the student friend of my gay student who was to be her spouse. If that sentence weren't true, why would I have written it?

After the phone calls to sort out that mess subsided — during which my two-year-old continued to announce his view that I shouldn't talk on the phone so much — my husband phoned from his hotel in New York to ask how things were at home. Then an old friend called from Dayton to announce that an even older (82) friend in Tucson had fallen, was in the hospital, was refusing to go to a nursing home, and was insisting on lesbian home care help. Surely I had a few contacts in Tucson. I did, so I called them. They seemed to be having the same sort of evening and were foolish enough to offer help.

I had planned to spend the evening mending.

35

Nine to Five

I couldn't stop thinking about the 9-to-5 day, about how much it got in the way of good, regular living. Women just wouldn't have the problems we have if we and our men weren't in that straitjacket, if we could work on a human timetable.

One hundred years ago as I write, 80,000 people marched in Chicago to demand the eight-hour day. Isn't that odd? They preferred the eight-hour day to the twelve-hour one. The Haymarket Centennial was a beautiful euphoria of the human spirit. We need another one.

Given that things were so politically quiet, I told myself I had better stop having these kinds of thoughts. They weren't productive. As we all know, being productive is of utmost importance. Having bizarre ideas that challenged uniformity would only cause depression, and then I would have to join all the other yuppies in getting a therapist to soothe my savaged soul.

Dinner at Home

All this commotion may have started at our dinner table. I didn't seem to know how to turn off the clock, even then. It only ticked louder when someone spilled their juice or refused to eat or fussed when they should have been fueling. Like many in this world, I made meals with a great appreciation for the quick and the instant. Things I or the kids would have enjoyed were ruled out for no other reason than the number of bowls or pots required for the preparation.

Dinner became a time to get through on our way to something better. Hurry it to the table and then hurry it to the disposal. Why? Dancing to the wrong drummer.

What could be better than a relaxed dinner with a family you love and whom you want to love you?

Fortunately, now I don't have a need for "TV Dinners" or their high-class descendants. I don't have to eat quickly because I have no place better to get.

(I wonder if I'll dare to add recipes to the final copy of this manifesto. There are many who would find a manifesto of freedom thereby trivialized.)

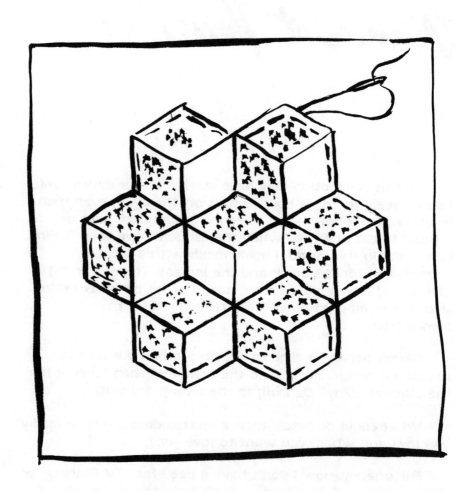

Quilt

When time is stolen, the thief is very quiet. It's like the time a thief took something out of the back of my car. I didn't even know it was gone for days. Then I went to look for it: SILENCE.

The same can be true of our history, our roots. Moving up is to become overly absorbed in the future. There's too much we have to forget on our climb.

I like to remember the absurd gatherings of my childhood: the ice skating, singing Zip-A-Dee-Doo-Dah. I like to remember the first kiss and touch of a boy, summer camp, softball games. Little thrills of accomplishment. I don't mind knowing that Joan Baez gives me goose bumps. I love the fact that I look like her. I like to remember how simple I thought things were on my first job.

That's why I started making quilts for the kids. Trains off the overalls, flannels from the jams, pictures of their old clothes that will tell the story of who they were.

I'll get as much pleasure securing memories for them as I do fondling my own.

The past has been stolen from too many of us. But there again, we gave it away.

Take back the night, we said, in one of my first political campaigns. Excellent slogan.

Meals you can't fix in a Hurry

The microwave may be our biggest problem. It cooks things too fast. Because it does a hard job with such ease, it tempts us to a mythology of ease.

Once we've decided we want to get rid of racism, we think we should be able to press a button. We have too little regard for history (like slavery), too little appreciation of generations (teen-agers on welfare giving birth to teen-agers who will be on welfare to repeat the cycle), and almost no sense of the web of systems that keep certain neighborhoods just the way they are. If our individual finger can't push to doneness, we are helpless. No wonder so many people ignore racism; if all you have is a hammer, all you see is nails. If all you have for help is individual haste, you can't bear to see problems that require collective slow-cook.

No wonder people with bad hearts can't stand to be around microwaves. They wore out their capacity to care long ago by having to live in a world that makes the natural working of the heart so difficult.

Retirement

The most exciting thing about growing up now rather than later is that I can stop thinking about retirement all the time. Retirement: when I'll tell people who offend me to buzz off. When I'll enjoy tea in the afternoon. When I'll read books, comic strips, and bad novels. When I'll get outside all the time, grow raspberries and keep the garden modestly weeded, clean out the closets, and make good soup out of leftover bones. Learn Spanish and have a flat tummy. Write poetic letters of appreciation to people who do hard work for low salaries and the opposite to dumbbells who pollute the airwaves on TV. See sunrises and sunsets. Make a quilt for every grandchild, like the ones I'll finish for my children, out of all their old clothes and favorite images. Enjoy a table set for two and figure out how to tell Warren how much I've loved him. Take the train through the Canadian Rockies, get sick of French bread with a perfect crust, get saturated with the sight of the ocean and red New England fall. Play cribbage and finish Shakespeare. Support people — particularly young ones — without telling them their business. Engage in all the civil disobedience that is necessary to stop the bomb and the way it grinds the face of the poor. Tell jokes and funny stories. Spend time doing none of the above, or nothing, or what someone I love wants to do.

Fortunately, I don't have to wait to get started living.

Physician, Heal Thyself

The funniest thing about doctors is the way they make their appointments — 5:10 6:40 7:10 etc. No regular hours for them. These weird numbers join doctors' fees to keep them in the position of Shamans. Who wouldn't wait two hours to see a Shaman or pay $35.00 for that privilege and the ten-minute cure written in bad handwriting? That scrawl is a crucial part of their costume.

Don't get me wrong. I'm the first one to rush to the waiting room when one of my children is sick.

But doctors drive me rapidly berserk. They are to health what microwaves are to the kitchen — quick fixes. As soon as they find out the type of insurance you have, they press the button of care suitable for your class. I live in a poor neighborhood but have a lot of money. For serious illnesses, I go twenty blocks south to get care that my money trusts; for regular illnesses, I go to the neighborhood clinic. Both make me wait; one gives twice the prescriptions of the other. Neither bothers to know my name or my children's names, and neither approaches my children with a gentle hand. Wham bang, thank you ma'am. No wonder my children are terrified of doctors: they should be.

Phony Shamans ARE terrifying. They hide their humanity and its limits behind their stethoscopes. I guess I'm the one who has to develop the bedside manner.

I'm also the one who is responsible for my health.

The Day Jacob was Sick

In my search to achieve normal human life, to cease the hyperconsciousness of modern living, to have a sense of being a regular person who has a tradition of maturing, I missed many clues. One was not understanding the normality of my upper West Side friend's son choosing the night of my annual visit to vomit his spaghetti dinner twice during our precious four hours of communication. The time was so structured; we had so much to say. He had so much to throw up. Maybe we're better friends today because we didn't have our "girl-talk" sharing then. Instead, I laundered her sheets and rugs, and kept her other child busy during a frightening, normal episode. We might have talked about HOW we live; instead, we just lived.

A second clue I missed, but won't miss again, was the day I canceled three important meetings to stay home with a sad, sick Jacob. Since our kids almost never got sick, I didn't get this opportunity very often. I thought I'd be mad. But instead, holding him all day and feeling his generous response, I found that a kind of healing was going on for me. It was good to miss something important in order to be with someone more important. The discovery of what mattered and what didn't made me feel regular and normal.

Sick kids contain many secrets.

Saul & Sigmund

I have an odd job — part teacher, part founder of a new school, part paid pioneer. I prepare seminarians, clergy, and lay people for public ministry. Usually I have to translate that to mean the time and space of transformation beyond soup kitchens and shelters, namely community organization and development. My job is to stay at the dash between nitty & gritty. HOW do we do the job of caring for the city? Close dying churches or reform them? Tolerate the gripers in every congregation or tell them good-bye? Feed the minister or get him/her to feed the congregation more? Fix the roof or fund the battered women's shelter? Ask us a question; we're supposed to develop an answer.

My mentors in this work are Saul Alinski and Sigmund Freud. What Freud did for psychoanalysis, Alinski did for community organizations. So, how is the personal political and the political personal? When is it which? What will it take to "restore streets to dwell in" for the United States in the 21st century? Will religious institutions contribute or get in the way? Will they matter?

Specifically, I teach the skills of community building, power analysis, and conflict resolution to people who are desperate to learn these things.

Saul says you can do these things in two years; Sigmund says five to seven. I get one night a month, a week, a summer, a semester.

It's taken me, already, all of my years, to get into a position to learn.

Answers become Questions

Other people think I know more than I do; they accuse me of answers.

Take welfare. I'd abolish it tomorrow if it were up to me. I know too many of its recipients to know that they're not helpless and hopeless. Plus, I hate social workers. The idea that they think they can help someone whose situation and class they only observe is preposterous.

Or cities. A lot of people say cities are dead. But that's because they didn't hear the saxophone on the corner of Broadway and Wilson that warm day in January.

Or "service professions." What a contradiction in terms. I love to teach ministers to be friends. Humble friends. And how to listen to the Blues.

This book is a personal project. But the object of its personal exercise is to get the power I need to hang on to the mystery of these questions. There is such a temptation to block out the mystery and think that clean closets and happy children will solve the questions.

They won't.

Interruptions

Being a woman is such a fragile thing. All plans contain an inferiority complex. They won't work for a spectrum of reasons, ranging all the way from another's need, that you might want to meet...to the intervention of power, a thing equally mysterious.

Maybe our lives are as interesting as the quality of the interruptions.

Once, when I thought I had this funky manifesto in a lovely shape, my father and my mother got sick, consecutively. I had to return to the haste of efficiency to make time for them. It seemed right to be tested.

Another time, long ago, I had to leave a college in the middle of the night. 1967. I was a white exchange student at a black college in the south. I was raped, and the dean's solution was to get me off campus as quickly as possible. That did not seem right.

Our lives are at the disposal of so many. Planning has to be very free — for good reasons and for disgusting ones.

I don't think life's interruptions will ever stop. Sometimes that makes me very sad. Other times I rejoice that I'm not a machine; and can never be programmed.

There's nothing like a change of pace to tell how important pace is.

Vintage

The real shift came for me when I started thinking of myself as an early feminist rather than a late feminist. Plowing new ground rather than old weeds. Early feminists have a right to sound weird. So what if I participate in the youth value that drives this culture; birth is too important a metaphor to let go.

Adrienne Rich complimented Emily Dickinson by referring to her as "half-cracked," choosing at last "to have it out on her own premises."

That is my situation, too. I will no longer let rape be something social services "fix." Sexual harassment will have to be a call to individual action and not a reason to form another support group. This me would not have left that college in the middle of the night. Right now I am personally organizing some friends to publicly accuse a well-known offender in the church. We've let him get away with it for too long.

Politeness is an overrated value. It keeps us from having it out on our own premises.

And that keeps us from growing up.

Reach out, Touch Someone

A friend of mine said her 40th birthday party was a flop because, just as it started, a friend of hers called, in tears, saying she'd just had an abortion. I understood. I have a lot of friends in trouble. Unemployed. Arrested for not paying their income taxes. Kids on drugs. On their way back to El Salvador. Divorcing. Disgusted. In love, out of love.

My friends are incredible people. They don't fool around — and even when they do, the fates of the middle time catch them, too. Most of us have stopped with the identity crisis and are full well into the midlife one. We don't even laugh about it anymore. Just because we're supposed to have one doesn't mean we won't; it works on the same bizarre rhythm as paranoia.

Some of my friends have made me sad by settling down. Others do the same thing and make me happy. Some sell out; others also buy in. But mostly they don't stop struggling, with one thing or another.

They warn me that there is no such thing as peace. There are only times when the struggle stops long enough so you can take a look around.

That's what I'm doing by writing this book. Looking around. Resting. So I can be stronger next time — or more content with my weakness. Or, at least, have enough spunk to call a friend. I can cry in private. I don't need meetings to stage my anguish.

The Helping Professions

What bothers me most about upward mobility is having secretaries and child care women, all of whom I employ at wages far less than mine. One is black and the other is Polish and a third is an older white woman who's been on welfare the last six years. It's uncanny how women like me are dependent on women like them.

Sisterhood is a strange phenomenon. My male co-workers are snide about the work the women in my office do. The men don't understand. Not women, not their own much-vaunted liberalism, not work. They don't understand how tricky it is to be a woman or how important it is to have eyes that look "down" as well as "up."

White women have astonishing choices. We can go either way — up to identify with men or down to remain with women. The old neighborhood we leave is typewriters and strollers, just like some blacks move out of Harlem and never return.

We have to be very careful. Our sexuality is the least of our worries. We have a little power, and power is SO easily abused.

61

Refusing Life to Save It

I always felt like my life was too much a disposal for fads: class of '65 high school and '69 college meant that I split for San Francisco just the right summer (of course with flowers in the hair); made it to Selma and Greensboro, and Washington for the Peace Marches. I had my first abortion the year it blew in and divorced at the peak of its popularity. Of course I belonged to consciousness-raising groups. Secaucus 7, the Big Chill, Woodstock all felt like my photo albums finally organized.

But I needed rest, time to grieve, time to assimilate into the human race.

Funny how the issues stay the same, even when the movements fade. My daughter, Katie, and I just went to a Pro-Choice rally. My speech was about the future: how I hoped we wouldn't have to miss supper because rights would be guaranteed. (Katie loves supper.)

But, for now, no matter how regular I yearn to be, some things are more important than supper.

Luxuries

I made bread and butter pickles one night soon after our twins were born. Here's the recipe. My mother gave it to me.

BREAD AND BUTTER PICKLES
4 qts. sliced cucumbers, 2 large onions, sliced, 2 red and 2 green peppers, cut in pieces, 4 tsp. salt, 1 tsp. dry mustard, 1 tsp. tumeric, 2 tsp. mustard seed, 3 cups sugar, 3 cups vinegar.

Let spices, sugar and vinegar come to a boil. Add sliced cucumbers, onions and peppers and bring to a boil again. Can hot.

Don't worry. I know you can buy them in the store. In this incredible city where I live, you can buy everything in the store. I frequently over-do the grocery shopping, so enamored am I of every little ethnic shop I've spotted.

The cucumbers were at the Farmer's Market at Lawrence and Western. $2.00 a bushel. My husband stayed up all night with me to make them. Another time in smelt season, some friends and I caught fish til three a.m. and made homemade french fries to go with them. By dawn we were full. We needed sleep. But we needed something else more.

The city has to be more than stores.

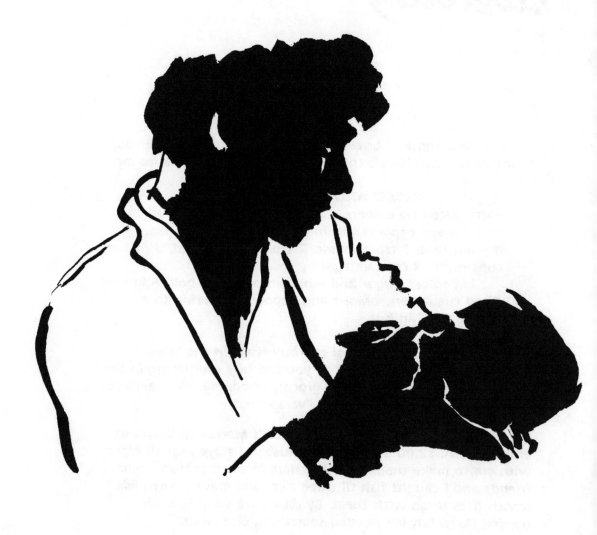

The Abstract Art of the Bathrobe

I have a beautiful white terry cloth robe that is thick and comfortable. I got it at a thrift shop for $2.50.

I laundered it with all the fancy products I could find — and it sparkled. I put it on the next morning with an air of achievement.

Jacob refused his Amoxicyllin and sprayed it all over my robed shoulder. Isaac decided on a hug, seconds following an encounter with blackberry jam. And Katie surreptitiously filled up her pants so that I didn't know their contents when I removed them to plunge her into the bath.

That's why brown, pink, and blackberry adorned my shoulder fifteen minutes after I put on my new robe.

How much more evidence do I need for the impurity of life?

The lengths to which I go for order and cleanliness are absurd. I can't stop, so I guess I'll have to learn to like color. The abstract art of the bathrobe.

If you want to know the truth, hard as I try, I can't keep my house clean either.

You should see the whoozies under the couch.

Toughness Test and Tears

What really amazed me about Geraldine Ferraro was that she never cried publicly during the campaign. You'd think she'd have better sense than that. Waiting in doctor's offices and leaving child care centers, I cry. Not out loud, just eyes misted over at wrong values. Tears that show me I still care about my time, even when it's the doctor's time which is supposed to be important. Tears for the child care worker who is much more important than my check to her will ever show.

I know people say Ferraro passed the toughness test. She could push a button if she had to. What that has to do with toughness is beyond me. And her marriage must be a mess. You'd think the Cardinal would have been impressed by her faithfulness to the covenant. But instead, he picked on her about abortion — more evidence of men's inability to see beyond their noses.

I hope she soaked her pillows when the cameras were off. Maybe the next time a woman runs for office, she'll be smart enough to show our grief in public; to show how, in addition to politics, we must be glue and shoestrings, child care worker, healer with the gentle bedside manner. Isn't it amazing, with all those jobs, that we would consider adding the job of politics?

Child Care

Shoestrings. That's what child care runs on. Shoestrings. At home, women use that awful word "just" to describe being a housewife. Outside the home, other women get a pittance per hour to take care of children. I visited a lot of child care centers, subsidized and non-subsidized, profit and not-for-profit, big and little, clean and dirty. I wanted a happy place for my children. Most of the children I saw knew how to be happy despite the little Egypt of their daily residence. It was the caretakers to whom Egypt was a pain. I always inquired about turnover of staff, just like Redbook's cute little guide advised me. Four to six months is the average stint of a child care worker. Many mothers would last only that long if they thought they had a choice.

Without shoestrings, shoes don't fit. The glue that "just a housewife" gives to husband and children is absolutely necessary to their well-being. It beats me that shoestrings and glue are so cheap when everything else is so expensive.

Don't worry. As soon as men get involved in child care, the price of shoestrings and glue will go up.

Ok. So worry. That day is not exactly on its way. Nor will it ever come if some of us don't cause its arrival. No one else but us can walk out of Egypt.

Dressing

When I'm in a really radical mood, I think about clothes. About what to wear. My feet, while looking good, have been killing me for years. I give society the right to expect something more than flannel nightgowns on the street and thus have combed mail order magazines, fashion magazines, department store racks, specialty shops, and pattern counters for clothes. To wear. Comfortably. They're all either too old or too young, too expensive or too cheap, too frilly or too macho. It's not just thrift that causes me to buy only in thrift shops. There the style is sufficiently eclectic enough to garb the executive earth-mother that I appear to be. I wish I had a dollar for every hour I've looked at clothes to express the real me. I'd be rich enough to custom order. I thought natural fibers would do it when they became the rage. But they became too much of a rage. I felt like I was saying too much about class and too little about cotton, linen, and wool.

Anyway, I dress like a college student. I wear too many socks. My wardrobe is understandably worn.

But at least I'm not uncomfortable anymore. And I'm not ready to go to flannel nightgowns or corduroys completely.

I retain a respect for social convention. Radicals can't be everything they want to be at once.

The Moving Bicycle

All two of my ideas to change the world rest on something simple — a bicycle.

One idea is to issue a bicycle to every man, woman, and child in the world. That displaces cars, concrete highways, the steel industry, the Middle East problem, and acid rain.

It also puts the diet book industry out of business.

The other is more subtle and connected to the first: don't let anyone move. Everyone can and should travel to different places. But they have to live where they are, with mom, dad, and noisy neighbors. Then maybe we'd learn to get along. This innovation would kick upward mobility right where it needs to be kicked. Ghettos would have to be cleaned up by the people who live there. Nursing homes would be abolished.

Plus, you would get where you needed on a bike, saving airplanes as shelters for the homeless.

The bicycle would make the diet easy. Staying home would provide the exercise.

Rest Now — You may not have time later

So superwoman intends to grow up. But she can't stop there. Not yet. It makes it too easy for those who now use their power in ways that don't care.

Probably our exodus is one that requires a trip to fatigue. We can't rest from caring. Yet. But we can rest in caring. And maybe our peace — in their chaos — will be the sign that will call the policymakers to care as well. We won't have to be the only tired ones — or tired forever.

We can rest wherever we want to. We have the freedom and the power to take care of ourselves and each other.

No amount of effort can take away what's already given.

More work won't achieve more grace.

Birthdays

Two years after I began this book, and a broken right wrist later, I've finished. I'm 40 now, going back to parish ministry in the state of my birth, New York. The government has not issued the bicycles, and I've moved again, leaving Chicago for the second time.

Maturity is probably more fun on the way than being there. Just as dreading the arrival of 40 was more horrifying than its arrival.

We had chocolate cake. I had two pieces. My whole family, and Warren's too, traveled to the beach house where we had the party. My mother put the candles on the cake — the three we used when I was a girl, German-made animal and childish figurines. For all the rest, she used the kind that don't blow out, no matter the effort.

Funny lady, my mother. At 63, she has kept her capacity to care, not once needing to write or read my manifesto on same.

the Author

Donna Schaper

When you look at Donna Schaper's credentials — a master's degree in religion from the University of Chicago; a Master of Divinity from Lutheran Theological Seminary (Gettysburg, PA); former Associate Chaplain at Yale; founder of Women Organized Against Rape (WOAR) in Philadelphia; Executive Director of Urban Academy in Chicago — it comes as no surprise to learn that she is currently the pastor of the First Congregational Church in Riverhead, New York, and a consultant at Union Seminary where she trains supervisors of seminarians.

What may be unexpected is Donna herself. Although she describes her life as undramatically bourgeois — "I have a dog, a cat, a mortgage, a husband; and all three of my children started nursery school yesterday" — she is a woman with many diverse skills and interests. In addition to pastoring, writing, and teaching, she also grows great strawberries, savors Paris, collects vestments, and claims to have "the world's largest telephone bill" in keeping up her connections with a network of close women friends.

the Artist

Maryam Gossling

Maryam Gossling brings to her artwork a variety of experience. Her background includes degrees in art education from Viterbo College (La Crosse, Wisconsin) and Ohio State University, and an MFA in painting and printmaking from the University of Wisconsin. She has taught art in schools in Iowa and Wisconsin and is currently working as a graphic artist in Los Angeles.

Maryam also has a certificate in Creation Spirituality from the Institute of Culture and Creation Spirituality, Holy Names College (Oakland, California). She is co-founder of Franciscan Canticle, Inc., a community of men and women artists who share the vision of St. Francis, with the desire to promote the word of God through the use of their gifts and talents.

When she is not illustrating books, Maryam loves to cook (she makes a great cheesecake!), read mysteries and science fiction, and experiment with Sumi painting.